Editor
Eric Migliaccio

Editor in Chief
Karen J. Goldfluss, M.S. Ed.

Creative Director
Sarah M. Fournier

Cover Artist
Barb Lorseyedi
Marilyn Goldberg

Illustrator
Donna Bizjak

Art Coordinator
Renée Mc Elwee

Imaging
James Edward Grace
Craig Gunnell

Publisher
Mary D. Smith, M.S. Ed.

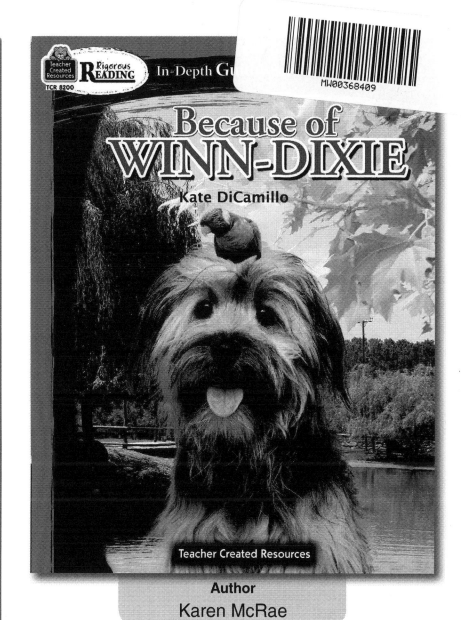

Because of
WINN-DIXIE

Kate DiCamillo

In-Depth Guide

Rigorous READING

TCR 8200

Teacher Created Resources

Author
Karen McRae

Teacher Created Resources
12621 Western Avenue
Garden Grove, CA 92841
www.teachercreated.com

ISBN: 978-1-4206-8200-7

© 2016 Teacher Created Resources
Made in U.S.A.

Teacher Created Resources

TABLE OF CONTENTS

TABLE OF CONTENTS (CONT.)

✦ ✦

INTRODUCTION

Read through the Common Core Standards for "Reading: Literature," and you will find that the work expected of students is expressed using such academic terminology as *describe*, *determine*, *develop*, *support*, and *cite*. Requirements such as these cannot be met via the comprehension-question worksheets and culminating quizzes that have long been the staples of literature guides designed for classroom use. The primary objective of those traditional activities was to make sure that students were keeping track of what was happening in the section of the novel that they had just read. Very little rigor and synthesis was asked of students—and usually none until the entire novel was read.

From a teacher's standpoint, this style of classroom analysis misses multiple opportunities to delve deeply into the details that make a specific piece of literature a classic; from a student's standpoint, this way to reflect on literature is monotonous and inflexible, and it fails to nurture the momentum experienced when one is invested in a compelling work of art. That is why the guides in the *Rigorous Reading* series aim to do much more: they aim to transform the reading of a great novel into a journey of discovery for students.

Instead of merely asking students what happened in any given section, this resource asks questions that require closer reading and deeper analysis—questions such as, "Why did the author choose to include this information?" and "How does this information further the plot or offer more insight into the themes, characters, settings, etc.?" And instead of waiting until the end of the novel to put the pieces of the puzzle in place, students will learn to add to and alter their understanding of the novel *as they are reading it*. The various activities in this resource systematically prompt students to consider and appreciate the many ingredients the author has combined to form the novel as a whole.

A CUSTOM RESOURCE

This in-depth guide has been written specifically for Kate DiCamillo's *Because of Winn-Dixie*. The lessons and activities have been structured and scaffolded to maximize the experience of reading and teaching this novel.

To prepare your students for their reading of *Because of Winn-Dixie*, utilize the **novel information** and **pre-reading activities** included on pages 7–9 of this guide. Included in this section is information about the book and its author, along with activities designed to acclimate students to the themes and/or concepts present in the book they are about to read.

This resource provides activities that help foster comprehension and reinforce knowledge of literary elements as students read *Because of Winn-Dixie*. These **section activities** allow students the opportunity to process short sections of the novel individually, laying a strong foundation for their ability to engage more deeply with the chapters to come. For each section of the novel, students will complete individual and collaborative activities that encourage close reading, referencing textual evidence, and drawing their own conclusions about the text.

Additionally, this resource provides students with another avenue through which they can reflect on recurring literary elements, while also connecting personally with the novel. Each student maintains his or her own **Interactive Novel Log**, using it as a way to consider and then reconsider various aspects of the novel.

Upon completion of the entire novel, students can synthesize their ideas about the novel by completing several individual and/or collaborative **post-reading activities** (pages 56–73). This section of the resource includes such larger assignments as group projects and essay assignments.

On pages 74–75, **vocabulary** lists are provided for each section of the novel, along with suggestions for ways to teach vocabulary during reading and after completing the novel.

At the end of this guide, an **answer key** is provided for activities that require specific answers, and a list identifies how each activity correlates to **Common Core State Standards**.

Key Notes

For a description of Interactive Novel Logs and how to use them in your classroom, see page 5 of this guide.

An ideal way to use this resource would be to follow the complete lesson plan given on page 6 of this guide.

The use of multiple texts can help build and extend knowledge about a theme or topic. It can also illustrate the similarities and differences in how multiple authors approach similar content or how an individual author approaches multiple novels. See the bottom of page 7 for suggestions about using *Because of Winn-Dixie* as part of a text set.

When teaching other novels in your classroom, consider using the specific ideas and also the general approach presented in this resource. Ask students to mine small sections of a novel for clues to theme and characterization. Examine the craft, structure, and purpose of select passages. Explore inferences and encourage connections.

This guide is designed for use in grades 3–6, and the standards correlations on pages 78–80 reflect this range. This leveling has been determined through the consideration of various educational metrics. However, teacher discretion should be used to determine if the novel and guide are appropriate for lower or higher grades, as well.

KEEPING NOVEL LOGS

Great works of literature are complex texts, and complex texts are multilayered. They enrich and reveal as they go along. Successful readers are those who "go along" with the novel, too. Interactive Novel Logs give students a place and a space to record their thoughts and observations as they journey through the book. After each section of the novel is read, students use their Interactive Novel Logs to track the introduction and development of such literary elements as plot, setting, theme, characterization, craft, and structure, while also choosing their own ways to connect the novel to their own life experiences.

Materials needed for each student:

✦ a three-ring binder or presentation folder

✦ a blank sheet of plain paper with holes punched for title page

✦ two or three sheets of blank lined paper for Table of Contents

✦ several extra sheets of paper (both lined and plain) for student's responses to the "Ideas for Your Interactive Log" prompts at the end of each section

> **Key Notes**
>
> One Interactive Novel Log can be kept for multiple novels, in which case a larger three-ring binder will be needed. If it will be used only for the activities included in this guide for *Because of Winn-Dixie*, a ½-inch binder or presentation folder will be adequate.

Assembling the Interactive Novel Log:

1. On the plain paper, allow students to design and decorate their own title page. Have them write "Interactive Novel Log" and "*Because of Winn-Dixie*" in the middle of the page. They should include their name and grade at the bottom.

2. Add blank lined paper for the Table of Contents. Have students write "Table of Contents" at the top. They will add to this list as they create new pages.

3. Before reading each section of the novel, photocopy and distribute new copies of the Interactive Novel Log worksheets (pages 10–15). Directions for completing these activities can be found in the "Teacher Instructions" that begin Section I.

4. For the final activity in each section, photocopy and distribute the "Section Log-In" page for the section. Follow the directions given. Students select one or more of the four topics in the "Ideas for Your Interactive Log" section and create an Interactive Novel Log page that responds to that topic.

5. After the class has completed the entire novel and the post-reading activities, you may have students include the "My Book Rating" worksheet (page 73) as a final entry in their Interactive Novel Logs.

COMPLETE LESSON PLAN

The following lesson plan presents a systematic way to use this entire guide in your classroom study of *Because of Winn-Dixie* by Kate DiCamillo.

Lesson 1

✦ Before students have begun reading the book, have them complete "Judging a Book" (page 8).

✦ Read "About the Author" (page 7) to the students. Have a discussion with students about their expectations for the novel based on the book's cover and what they know about its author.

✦ Complete "Summer in Your Town" (page 9).

✦ Introduce the concept of Interactive Novel Logs (see page 5). Prepare a blank notebook for each student or allow students to prepare their own.

Lesson 2

✦ Read Section I (Chapters 1–4) of the novel.

✦ See Section I "Teacher Instructions" (page 16). Have students add to their Novel Logs before completing the other Section I activities.

Lesson 3

✦ Read Section II (Chapters 5–7) of the novel.

✦ See Section II "Teacher Instructions" (page 22). Have students add to their Novel Logs before completing the other Section II activities.

Lesson 4

✦ Read Section III (Chapters 8–11) of the novel.

✦ See Section III "Teacher Instructions" (page 27). Have students add to their Novel Logs before completing the other Section III activities.

Lesson 5

✦ Read Section IV (Chapters 12–15) of the novel.

✦ See Section IV "Teacher Instructions" (page 32). Have students add to their Novel Logs before completing the other Section IV activities.

Lesson 6

✦ Read Section V (Chapters 16–19) of the novel.

✦ See Section V "Teacher Instructions" (page 38). Have students add to their Novel Logs before completing the other Section V activities.

Lesson 7

✦ Read Section VI (Chapters 20–23) of the novel.

✦ See Section VI "Teacher Instructions" (page 43). Have students add to their Novel Logs before completing the other Section VI activities.

Lesson 8

✦ Read Section VII (Chapters 24–26) of the novel.

✦ See Section VII "Teacher Instructions" (page 50). Have students add to their Novel Logs before completing the other Section VII activities.

Lesson 9

✦ Consult "Teacher Instructions" (page 56).

✦ Synthesize understanding by completing the first four Post-Reading Activities (pages 57–61).

✦ Allow students to reimagine the text by completing "A New Point of View" (page 62) and "Considering Genre" (page 63).

✦ Complete larger-scale collaborative (pages 64–67) and individual (68–71) projects.

✦ Have students share final thoughts and opinions on the novel with the last two Post-Reading Activities (pages 72–73).

✦ Consider additional vocabulary-based activities (pages 74–75).

NOVEL INFORMATION

Book Summary

Because of Winn-Dixie is a Newbery Honor Award novel that tells the story of 10-year-old Opal, a girl with a lot of personality but not a lot of friends. She lost her mother at a young age, and she has just lost everything else familiar because her father moved her to to the town of Naomi, Florida, so he could become the preacher for a local church.

Just when Opal feels like she will never make a single friend, Winn-Dixie comes into her life. A dog who smiles frequently and makes friends easily, Winn-Dixie is just what Opal needs. Because of her new pet, Opal meets and befriends a diverse group of people who are as interesting and as in need of something new as she is. Through this newfound community, Opal learns to accept the past and embrace the future.

About the Author

Born on March 25, 1964, Kate DiCamillo was ill for much of her childhood. As a result, she moved along with her mother and brother to the warmer weather of Florida when she was five. Her father did not come along with the family.

In her early 30s, DiCamillo began writing children's literature. Her first novel, *Because of Winn-Dixie*, was published in 2000. It was an immediate success, and it earned her a Newbery Honor Award. Two of her later novels — *The Tale of Despereaux* (2003) and *Flora and Ulysses* (2013) — were each awarded Newbery Medals. All three novels feature important animal characters.

Make It a Text Set!

The following novels can form ideal text sets with *Because of Winn-Dixie*. (**Note:** Vet books in advance to ensure they are appropriate for your students.)

Other Novels by Kate DiCamillo	Books by Other Authors
The Tiger Rising (2001)	*Tales of a Fourth Grade Nothing* by Judy Blume
The Tale of Despereaux (2003)	*The One and Only Ivan* by Katherine Applegate
Flora & Ulysses: The Illuminated Adventures (2013)	*A Dog's Life* by Ann Martin

NAME: _____

JUDGING A BOOK

You are about to read a novel named *Because of Winn-Dixie*. Before you even pick up the book and look at it, answer these questions.

1. Have you heard of the novel *Because of Winn-Dixie* before? ☐ YES ☐ NO

   If **YES**, then explain what you have heard or already know about this novel.

   _____

   _____

2. Think about the title of the book. Based on the title, what do you expect the tone of the novel to be? Place a checkmark next to any or all.

   ☐ adventurous   ☐ funny   ☐ heartwarming   ☐ sad

   ☐ scary   ☐ silly   ☐ heartbreaking   ☐ tense

   Explain your choices(s) here.

   _____

   _____

Now pick up the book. You have probably heard the saying, "Don't judge a book by its cover," but let's do it anyway.

3. Briefly describe the colors on the front of the book.

   _____

   _____

4. Briefly describe the images on the front of the book.

   _____

   _____

   _____

5. In a few sentences, describe the mood evoked by the color and images on the front of the book. In other words, based on these two elements, what impressions and feelings do you have about the book you are about to read?

   _____

   _____

   _____

NAME: _____

SUMMER IN YOUR TOWN

The novel you are about to read takes place during the summer. In this novel, 10-year-old Opal adapts to life in Naomi, Florida.

Before you begin reading about Opal's summer, think about the summers in your town.

1. In which state/province/area do you live? _____

2. In your town, what is the weather like during the summer? Be descriptive.

    _____

3. Which people (other than family) do you see a lot during the summer?

    _____

4. Which places in town do you go a lot during the summer?

    _____

    _____

5. Choose three words to describe a typical summer day in your town.

Word	Why You Chose This Word

6. Create timelines of typical summer mornings and afternoons for you in your town.

Time (A.M.)					
What You Are Doing					

Time (P.M.)					
What You Are Doing					

NAME: _____

THE SUMMARIES OF ITS PARTS

As you finish reading each section of *Because of Winn-Dixie*, take a few minutes to summarize the events that have taken place. Use the following tips to guide you.

Tips for Writing Summaries

+ **Focus only on the most important events.** Do not include extra details or examples. A summary should be a quick retelling of only the major plot points.

+ **Use your own words.** Do not quote words directly from the novel.

+ **Use transition words.** Words and phrases like *first*, *next*, *then*, *after that*, and *finally* quickly show the sequence in which events occur in the novel.

Fit your summary on the lines provided below.

+ +

Summary for Section #: _____   **Chapters in this section:** _____

Page numbers in this section: *from page* _____ *to page* _____

+ +

_____

_____

_____

_____

_____

_____

_____

_____

In one or two complete sentences, name the single thing you found most interesting in this chapter. Your answer can be about something that happened in the plot, the way a character reacted to an event, or the way the author chose to write a particular line.

_____

_____

_____

MAJOR MINORS

Because of Winn-Dixie has one major character. Her name is Opal, and she is the one who is telling us about herself and everyone else. The novel is written from her perspective.

However, the novel has many minor characters. These characters are important, too. As you read each section of the novel, write a little bit about each character that is introduced in that section. Write the character's name and how Opal meets him or her. Also try to answer this question about the character: Why might he or she be included in the novel? You most likely will not know the true answer at this point, so just give your best guess.

+ +

Section #: _____   **Chapters in this section:** _____

Page numbers in this section: *from page* _____ *to page* _____

+ +

Character Introduced	How Opal Meets Him or Her	Why He or She Is in the Novel

NAME: _____

BECAUSE OF THE TITLE

The novel you are reading is titled *Because of Winn-Dixie.* Only a few pages into the novel, we learn who Winn-Dixie is. As you read each section, think about how some of the events in the novel happen "because of Winn-Dixie."

+ +

Section #: _____   **Chapters in this section:** _____

Page numbers in this section: *from page* _____ *to page* _____

+ +

Write about two events that take place in the section you have just read.

Event #1

What happens? _____

_____

_____

How does it happen "because of Winn-Dixie"? Explain your answer.

_____

_____

_____

What does this event change for Opal? _____

_____

_____

Event #2

What happens? _____

_____

_____

How does it happen "because of Winn-Dixie"? Explain your answer.

_____

_____

_____

What does this event change for Opal? _____

_____

_____

CHECKING IN ON THEME

Because of Winn-Dixie is full of themes that appear and reappear throughout its 26 chapters. A theme is a message behind the story.

Look below at this list of themes. Choose one that you think is very important to this section. Put a checkmark in the box next to that theme.

✦ ✦

Section #: _____   **Chapters in this section:** _____

Page numbers in this section: *from page* _____ *to page* _____

✦ ✦

Themes

- ❑ **Abandonment** (being left behind by someone or something)
- ❑ **Acceptance** (learning to accept people for who they are and not judge them)
- ❑ **Communication** (understanding others and being understood)
- ❑ **Courage** (being strong enough to be yourself and to move forward)
- ❑ **Friendship** (forming bonds with other people or animals)
- ❑ **Loneliness** (feeling alone in the world)

Why did you think this theme was the most important in this section? Write a paragraph in which you explain your choice. Use at least two examples from the section chapters.

_____

_____

_____

_____

_____

_____

_____

_____

_____

_____

NAME: _____

CHOICE WORDS

+ +

Word from Novel: _____ **From Chapter #:** _____

+ +

1. Find one quotation in which this word appears in the novel. Write it in the box.

> [box]

2. Reread the paragraph or section that contains the vocabulary word. Consider what is happening in the story and how the author uses the word. This information can help you figure out its meaning. Based on the words and ideas around the word, what do you think is its meaning?

_____

_____

3. Explain why you think this is the meaning of the word, based on the context.

_____

_____

_____

4. Now look up the word in the dictionary and write down the definition of this word that best fits the way it is used in the novel.

_____

_____

5. What is the part of speech of this word as it is used in the novel? _____

6. Next, look up the word in the thesaurus and write at least one synonym and one antonym of the word.

Synonym(s): _____   Antonym(s): _____

_____   _____

7. Write your own sentence that uses the vocabulary word.

_____

_____

NAME: _____

CRYSTAL BALL

Now that you have read this section, where do you think the story will go next? Make two predictions based on what you have read so far. They can be about any of the following:

✦ **plot** — What will happen next in the story?

✦ **characterization** — What changes will Opal or other characters undergo?

✦ **theme** — What big ideas about life, survival, etc., will the author explore?

Use details from previous sections to explain why you are making each prediction.

✦ + ✦

Section #: _____   **Chapters in this section:** _____

Page numbers in this section: *from page* _____ *to page* _____

✦ + ✦

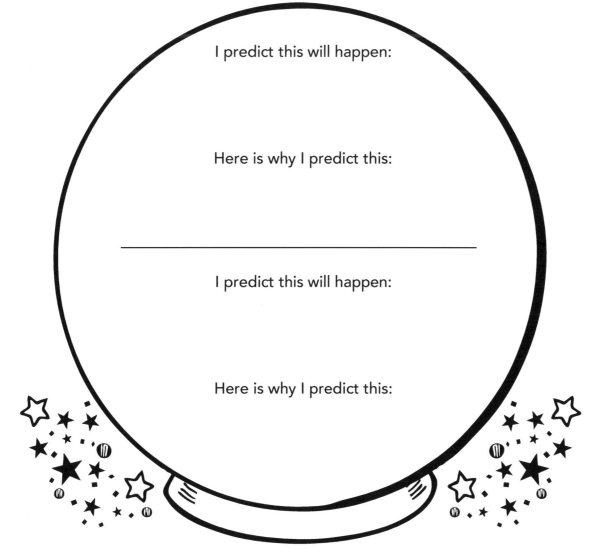

I predict this will happen:

Here is why I predict this:

_____

I predict this will happen:

Here is why I predict this:

TEACHER INSTRUCTIONS

The first four chapters of this novel introduce us to the three main characters—Opal, her father, and her new pet—and show us how each needs a fresh start in life.

After your students have read Chapters 1–4, have them begin their analyses of this section of the novel by completing the following activities for their Interactive Novel Logs. Each of these activities is to be done individually.

+ **"The Summaries of Its Parts"** on page 10. Ensure that students read the directions carefully and understand what does and does not belong in a summary.

+ **"Major Minors"** on page 11. Read the directions to students. Stress that not all of the rows in the chart need to be filled out.

+ **"Because of the Title"** on page 12. If you choose, allow students to write about more than two events from this section. Use extra paper, as needed.

+ **"Checking In on Theme"** on page 13. Be sure the students understand the concept of theme before beginning this activity.

+ **"Choice Words"** on page 14. Assign one or more words from "Novel Vocabulary" (page 75) or allow students to choose their own word(s).

+ +

Students will then further examine this section through the following worksheets:

Activity: "The Storyboard of How They Met" **Page #:** 17
Focus: Plot, Craft and Structure **Learning Type:** Individual
Description: Use a storyboard to visually represent the opening scene of the novel. Consider the individual moments that make up this scene and determine why this scene is an effective choice to open the novel.

Activity: "Finding a Friend" **Page #:** 18
Focus: Plot, Characterization **Learning Type:** Collaborative
Description: With a partner, examine the traits of Winn-Dixie and decide why these traits were so appealing to Opal.

Activity: "A Turtle in Its Shell" **Page #:** 19
Focus: Characterization, Craft and Structure **Learning Type:** Individual
Description: Locate the author's use of metaphor in a key character description. Explain why the author might have chosen to use this literary device.

Activity: "Different and Alike" **Page #:** 20
Focus: Characterization **Learning Type:** Individual
Description: Analyze the three characters that are the focus of this section. Compare and contrast them.

Activity: "Section I Log-In" **Page #:** 21
Focus: Plot, etc. **Learning Type:** Individual
Description: Complete "Crystal Ball" worksheets in order to predict future events in the novel. Then choose from several options to add to Interactive Novel Logs.

THE STORYBOARD OF HOW THEY MET

Because of Winn-Dixie begins with an important scene: the meeting of Opal and Winn-Dixie. Create a **storyboard** to show this scene. To do this, draw pictures of six key moments in the scene. You may use a few words in each, but try to tell the story of the scene mostly through images.

1.	2.	3.
4.	**5.**	**6.**

✦ ✦

Considering Craft

Why do you think the author chose to start the book with this scene? As a reader, how well does this scene draw you into the book and make you want to read more?

_____

_____

_____

_____

NAME(S): _____

FINDING A FRIEND

In the previous activity, you drew a storyboard to show what happened in the scene where Opal meets Winn-Dixie. This meeting sets up the rest of the novel.

Why do you think Opal wanted to take Winn-Dixie home with her? What about this dog appealed to her? With a partner, complete this chart and answer the questions below.

Things about Winn-Dixie that most people might like.	Things about Winn-Dixie that most people might not like.

1. Do you think most people would want to take Winn-Dixie home with them? Why or why not?

   _____

   _____

   _____

2. Right away, Opal knows she likes Winn-Dixie. What three things do you think she most liked about the dog immediately?

   a. _____

   b. _____

   c. _____

3. What might it say about Opal that she liked these three things about Winn-Dixie enough to take him home?

   _____

   _____

   _____

NAME: _____

A TURTLE IN ITS SHELL

In Chapter 2 of *Because of Winn-Dixie*, Opal describes her father as a turtle with a shell. Find the first time Opal describes him this way. Write the quotation in the box.

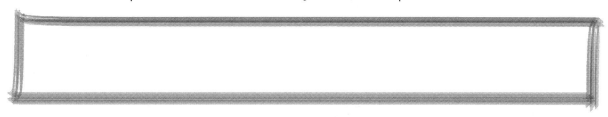

A **metaphor** is a figure of speech that people use when they write or speak. A metaphor compares two unlike things. It says that even though these two things are very *un*alike in most ways, they are very alike in at least one way.

1. How is Opal's father very *unlike* a turtle? (Don't think too hard on this one!)

   _____

2. According to Opal, how is her father very much *like* a turtle?

   _____

   _____

   _____

3. What does being like a turtle in this way tell us about Opal's father?

   _____

   _____

   _____

4. How is Opal using a metaphor in the quotation you wrote in the box above?

   _____

   _____

   _____

5. Why do you think the author of this novel has Opal use a metaphor to describe her father? Why might she do this instead of just telling us what Opal's father is like?

   _____

   _____

   _____

   _____

NAME: _____

DIFFERENT AND ALIKE

In Chapters 1–4 of *Because of Winn-Dixie*, we mostly meet three characters. Think of three words to describe each character. If any of those words also describe one of the other characters, fill in the bubble below that character's name.

Three Words to Describe Opal	Three Words to Describe the Preacher	Three Words to Describe Winn-Dixie
1. _____ Could this word describe ○ the preacher? ○ Winn-Dixie?	**1.** _____ Could this word describe ○ Opal? ○ Winn-Dixie?	**1.** _____ Could this word describe ○ Opal? ○ the preacher?
2. _____ Could this word describe ○ the preacher? ○ Winn-Dixie?	**2.** _____ Could this word describe ○ Opal? ○ Winn-Dixie?	**2.** _____ Could this word describe ○ Opal? ○ the preacher?
3. _____ Could this word describe ○ the preacher? ○ Winn-Dixie?	**3.** _____ Could this word describe ○ Opal? ○ Winn-Dixie?	**3.** _____ Could this word describe ○ Opal? ○ the preacher?

+ +

Considering Characterization

How are these three characters most alike? In these first four chapters, what do they most have in common?

_____

_____

_____

_____

_____

NAME: _____

SECTION 1 LOG-IN

Now that you have finished the activities for this section of *Because of Winn-Dixie*, take some time to add to your Interactive Novel Log before you begin reading the next section.

✦ **First, make a prediction about what will happen next in the novel.**

Use your "Crystal Ball" worksheet (page 15) to do this.

✦ **Next, make a more personal connection to what you have read.**

Choose one of the suggestions below and use it to fill a page in your Interactive Novel Log. Take this opportunity to connect with the novel in a way that appeals to you.

✦ + ✦

Ideas for Your Interactive Novel Log

1
A New Place

Have you ever moved to a new town, just as Opal does in *Because of Winn-Dixie*? What was it like? And if you haven't, think about what it would be like. Divide your notebook page into two columns (see below) and fill out each column. Show what was (or would be) both good and bad about moving to a new town.

Top 5 Things That Were (or Would Be) Hard	Top 5 Things That Were (or Could Be) Good
1.	1.
2.	2.
3.	3.
4.	4.
5.	5.

2
A New Pet

When Opal spots Winn-Dixie in the supermarket, she knows she wants to take that dog home with her. What would make you want to take a dog or other pet home with you? What kind of an animal would you want it to be? Draw an outline shape of your new pet. Inside the shape, write five things that explain what would make the perfect pet for you.

3
Ten About You

Opal asks her father to tell her 10 things about her mother. Imagine you are asked to say 10 things about yourself. Write your list of 10. Add drawings or photos to illustrate some of your list.

4
Ten About Another

Imagine you are asked to provide a list of 10 things about someone else. Choose a family member or a famous person you look up to. Write your list of 10. Add drawings or photos to illustrate some of your list.

TEACHER INSTRUCTIONS

In this section of *Because of Winn-Dixie*, Opal gets to know her new pet and makes a new human friend, too.

After your students have read Chapters 5–7, have them begin their analyses of this section of the novel by completing the following activities for their Interactive Novel Logs. Each of these activities is to be done individually.

✦ **"The Summaries of Its Parts"** (page 10)

✦ **"Major Minors"** (page 11)

✦ **"Because of the Title"** (page 12)

✦ **"Checking In on Theme"** (page 13)

✦ **"Choice Words"** (page 14)

> *For this section, distribute new copies of the Interactive Novel Log worksheets on pages 10–14.*

✦ ✦

Students will then further examine this section through the following worksheets:

Activity: "Setting the Tone" **Page #:** 23
Focus: Craft and Structure **Learning Type:** Individual
Description: Determine the tone of the church scene from Chapter 5 and how the author achieved this tone through the various elements included in the scene.

Activity: "Infer the Information" **Page #:** 24
Focus: Craft and Structure **Learning Type:** Individual
Description: Analyze how the author gives clues and allows readers to use inference to interpret a character's point of view.

Activity: "What's the Big Idea?" **Page #:** 25
Focus: Plot **Learning Type:** Collaborative
Description: With a partner, examine how each chapter in this section is its own small story with its own main idea. Practice speaking and listening skills for the first two chapters in the section, and then work together to decide on the main idea of Chapter 7.

Activity: "Section II Log-In" **Page #:** 26
Focus: Plot, etc. **Learning Type:** Individual
Description: Complete "Crystal Ball" worksheets in order to predict future events in the novel. Then choose from several options to add to Interactive Novel Logs.

NAME: _____

SETTING THE TONE

Most of Chapter 5 involves a scene that takes place in a church. After reading this scene, what would you say is the tone? Is it funny, silly, sad, serious, or something else?

Use your answer to complete the chart below. The column on the left lists four elements that the author combined to create this chapter. For each of these elements, explain how it contributed to the tone of Chapter 5.

Element	How It Contributed to the Tone
Plot (the events that happen)	
Setting (the place where the events happen)	
Characterization (the people and animals in the story)	
Voice (the tone of the narrator who is telling the story)	

In your opinion, which of these elements — Plot, Setting, Characterization, or Voice — was the most important for the setting the tone of this scene? Check the box next to your answer, and then explain your choice on the lines below.

❑ Plot   ❑ Setting   ❑ Characterization   ❑ Voice

_____

_____

_____

_____

_____

NAME: _____

INFER THE INFORMATION

In this section of the novel, we meet the character of Miss Franny Block. Since *Because of Winn-Dixie* is a story told by Opal, we get to read Opal's thoughts during the scenes that take place in the Herman W. Block Memorial Library. This is not the case with Miss Block, however. We don't know exactly what she is thinking, and she doesn't usually state this information directly. We have to use inference. We have to infer this information from her actions.

> To **infer** something is to figure it out by combining clues provided in the text with things you already know.

Use inference to answer the following questions.

1. When Winn-Dixie comes into the library — after Miss Block realizes that he's not a bear — what is Miss Block's first reaction to him? Write about what Miss Block says and does to Winn-Dixie.

_____

_____

2. When Miss Block finishes her bear story, what does Winn-Dixie do to her?

_____

3. How does Miss Block respond to this? How does it seem to make her feel?

_____

_____

4. When Amanda enters the library, what does she tell Miss Block?

_____

_____

5. How does Miss Block respond to what Amanda says?

_____

_____

6. Based on what you have answered, can you infer how Miss Block feels about Winn-Dixie and Amanda? Support your opinion with clues from the text.

_____

_____

_____

WHAT'S THE BIG IDEA?

Because of Winn-Dixie is organized into 26 short chapters. Together, the chapters tell the whole story; by themselves, each chapter tells a smaller story. Often, a line or phrase from the chapter announces the main idea of that smaller story.

With a partner, examine the main ideas of Chapters 5, 6, and 7. Begin by deciding who will be Speaker 1 and who will be Speaker 2. Then follow the chart.

	Speaker 1	Speaker 2
Name		
Speaking Assignment	Read the first line from Chapter 5 aloud to Speaker 2. Explain why the phrase "Winn-Dixie couldn't stand to be left alone" is the main idea of this chapter. Give several examples of how the meaning of this phrase is illustrated by the events that occur in Chapter 5.	Read the last line of the first paragraph from Chapter 6 aloud to Speaker 1. Explain why the phrase "she was the first friend I made in Naomi" is the main idea of this chapter. Give examples of how the meaning of this phrase is illustrated by the events that occur in Chapter 6.
Listening Assignment	Tell Speaker 2 if you agree or disagree with anything he or she said or if you feel that any good examples from Chapter 6 were not mentioned.	Tell Speaker 1 if you agree or disagree with anything he or she said or if you feel that any good examples from Chapter 5 were not mentioned.

Now as a team, locate an important quote from Chapter 7. Find the one that best illustrates the main idea of that chapter. Write it in the box.

How does this one quote best illustrate the main idea of Chapter 7?

_____

_____

_____

_____

NAME: _____

SECTION II LOG-IN

Now that you have finished the activities for this section of *Because of Winn-Dixie*, take some time to add to your Interactive Novel Log before you begin reading the next section.

✦ **First, make a prediction about what will happen next in the novel.**

Use your "Crystal Ball" worksheet (page 15) to do this.

✦ **Next, make a more personal connection to what you have read.**

Choose one of the suggestions below and use it to fill a page in your Interactive Novel Log. Take this opportunity to connect with the novel in a way that appeals to you.

+ +

Ideas for Your Interactive Novel Log

1
Buildings in Your Town

In Chapters 5 and 6, we are given descriptions of two important buildings in the town of Naomi: a church and the public library. Think about the buildings in your town. Choose one on which to focus. Draw a picture of the exterior (outside) of this building, then divide the rest of your page in half. On one side, describe what the interior (inside) of the building looks like. On the other side, explain why you chose to feature this building. Is it important to you? Does it have an interesting design? Do you think the visitors to your town would notice this building among all of the others?

2
Animal Adventures

Chapters 5 and 7 each tell a story about animals being inside buildings where they normally aren't allowed. Use your page to tell a story from your experiences. Describe a time when you saw an animal in a place where it usually wouldn't be.

3
Overdue Poster

Make an informative poster that can be displayed in the Herman W. Block Memorial Library. Your poster should give information about the creature that borrowed a book long ago and has yet to return it. Be sure to answer several of the 5Ws (who, what, where, when, and why) on your poster.

4
How It Makes Me Feel

Now that you have read seven full chapters of *Because of Winn-Dixie*, how does it make you feel so far? Create a page of words, pictures, and colors that describes the tone of these first seven chapters.

TEACHER INSTRUCTIONS

In this section of *Because of Winn-Dixie*, Opal gets a job, meets more of the local townspeople, and learns about Winn-Dixie's fear of thunderstorms.

After your students have read Chapters 8–11, have them begin their analyses of this section of the novel by completing the following activities for their Interactive Novel Logs. Each of these activities is to be done individually.

✦ **"The Summaries of Its Parts"** (page 10)

✦ **"Major Minors"** (page 11)

✦ **"Because of the Title"** (page 12)

✦ **"Checking In on Theme"** (page 13)

✦ **"Choice Words"** (page 14)

> For this section, distribute new copies of the Interactive Novel Log worksheets on pages 10–14.

✦ ✦

Students will then further examine this section through the following worksheets:

Activity: "So to Speak" **Page #:** 28
Focus: Characterization, Craft and Structure **Learning Type:** Collaborative
Description: Compare two exchanges of dialogue and determine what these interactions say about the characters involved.

Activity: "How You Know" **Page #:** 29
Focus: Plot, Craft and Structure **Learning Type:** Individual
Description: Provide textual evidence to show how the author sets up Opal's introduction to Gloria Dump.

Activity: "What the Storm Brings" **Page #:** 30
Focus: Plot **Learning Type:** Individual
Description: Examine the storm scene and how it reveals and alters the dynamic between the three main characters. Consider if the storm might foreshadow future events in the novel.

Activity: "Section III Log-In" **Page #:** 31
Focus: Plot, etc. **Learning Type:** Individual
Description: Complete "Crystal Ball" worksheets in order to predict future events in the novel. Then choose from several options to add to Interactive Novel Logs.

NAME(S): _____

SO TO SPEAK

Chapter 8 is filled with dialogue. There are two main exchanges: the first takes place inside Gertrude's Pets, while the second takes place outside the store. With a partner, examine each scene.

Exchange #1: Inside the Pet Store	Exchange #2: Outside the Pet Store
1. Which two characters are talking? _____ _____	**1.** Which two characters are talking? _____ _____
2. What is the dialogue mostly about? _____ _____ _____	**2.** What is the dialogue mostly about? _____ _____ _____
3. Look back at your answer to #1. Circle the name of the character who speaks the most during this scene.	**3.** Look back at your answer to #1. Circle the name of the character who speaks the most during this scene.
4. What do you think this scene says about Opal? Think about the amount of talking she does, why she says things the way she does, and how she interacts with the other person. _____ _____ _____ _____	**4.** What do you think this scene says about Opal? Think about the amount of talking she does, why she says things the way she does, and how she interacts with the other person. _____ _____ _____ _____
5. What do you think this scene says about the person speaking with Opal? _____ _____ _____	**5.** What do you think this scene says about the person speaking with Opal? _____ _____ _____

NAME: _____

HOW YOU KNOW

Chapter 9 introduces Opal and us readers to another of Naomi's citizens. Look at each part of the story to see how the author introduces each part of this small story.

1. How soon into Chapter 9 did you know what this chapter would be about?

   _____

   Quote a line that gave you this information: _____

   _____

2. What do some of the kids in town think of Gloria Dump?

   _____

   _____

   Quote a line that gave you this information: _____

   _____

3. How do the Dewberry boys know who Opal is? _____

   _____

   Quote a line that gave you this information: _____

   _____

4. Why does Opal go into Mrs. Dump's yard despite what the boys say?

   _____

   _____

   Quote a line that gave you this information: _____

   _____

5. Just from Chapter 9, how would you describe Mrs. Dump's personality?

   _____

   _____

   Quote two lines that gave you this information: _____

   _____

   _____

   _____

NAME: _____

WHAT THE STORM BRINGS

Review Chapter 11 and decide what it reveals about the three main characters.

1. What is the main event that takes place in Chapter 11? _____

_____

2. How does Winn-Dixie react to this event? _____

_____

_____

3. How does Opal react to Winn-Dixie's reaction? _____

_____

_____

4. How does Opal's father react to Winn-Dixie's reaction? _____

_____

_____

5. How does Opal react to her father's reaction? _____

_____

_____

6. Why do you think she reacts this way? Support your answer with a quotation.

_____

_____

_____

7. What does Opal's father say about Florida in the summer? Quote the line here.

_____

8. In light of the quotation from #7, how might this event change Opal's view of having Winn-Dixie as her pet? Explain.

_____

_____

_____

_____

NAME: _____

SECTION III LOG-IN

Now that you have finished the activities for this section of *Because of Winn-Dixie*, take some time to add to your Interactive Novel Log before you begin reading the next section.

✦ **First, make a prediction about what will happen next in the novel.**
Use your "Crystal Ball" worksheet (page 15) to do this.

✦ **Next, make a more personal connection to what you have read.**
Choose one of the suggestions below and use it to fill a page in your Interactive Novel Log. Take this opportunity to connect with the novel in a way that appeals to you.

+ +

Ideas for Your Interactive Novel Log

1
First Jobs

In Chapter 8, Opal gets what is most likely her first job. Divide your page into two spaces. In one, write about Opal's job: where it is, what she'll be doing, and what she hopes to pay for with the money she'll earn. On the other side of your page, write about a first job you might have some day. Answer the same questions as you did for Opal. If you've already had your first job, then write about that experience.

2
First Encounters

In Chapters 9 and 10, we read about Opal's first encounter with Gloria Dump. Write about a memorable first encounter that you had with someone who became an important part of your life. Include details such as what you were doing, what you were wearing, and where this encounter took place. Also describe your initial (first) impression of this person.

3
Seeing-Eye Heart

In Chapter 9, Gloria Dump says that her eyes do not work very well, and so she would like to see Opal with her heart. What do you think it means to see someone with your heart? Write a true story about when you saw someone with your heart, or make up a story about a character seeing another with his or her heart.

4
An Inconvenient Fear

Opal's father describes Winn-Dixie's reaction to the thunderstorm as a "pathological fear." He also says there are a lot of those storms where they live. Think about the weather or some other thing that occurs frequently where you live. What would be an inconvenient thing to have a pathological fear about in your part of the world? Make two lists. One should explain the thing that happens often in your area. The other should give reasons why it would be unfortunate to be afraid of that thing.

TEACHER INSTRUCTIONS

In this section of *Because of Winn-Dixie*, Opal spends time with and learns more about her new friends in town: Otis, Miss Franny, and Gloria Dump.

After your students have read Chapters 12–15, have them begin their analyses of this section of the novel by completing the following activities for their Interactive Novel Logs. Each of these activities is to be done individually.

(**Note:** Do not distribute the "Major Minors" worksheet, as no new minor characters are introduced in this section.)

✦ **"The Summaries of Its Parts"** (page 10)

✦ **"Because of the Title"** (page 12)

✦ **"Checking In on Theme"** (page 13)

✦ **"Choice Words"** (page 14)

> *For this section, distribute new copies of the Interactive Novel Log worksheets on pages 10, 12, 13, and 14.*

✦ ✦

Students will then further examine this section through the following worksheets:

Activity: "Acting Her Age?" **Page #:** 33
Focus: Characterization **Learning Type:** Collaborative
Description: With a partner, consider Opal's thoughts and actions in this section of the novel. Decide if any conclusions can be drawn about how Opal interacts with the characters around her.

Activity: "Character Close-Ups" **Page #:** 34–35
Focus: Plot, Craft and Structure **Learning Type:** Individual
Description: Catalog the new information Opal learns about six important characters in this section of the novel. Determine how this information informs Opal's view, as well as society's view, of these characters.

Activity: "The Big Old Tree" **Page #:** 36
Focus: Plot, Symbolism **Learning Type:** Individual
Description: Examine the passage about the tree in Gloria Dump's backyard. Provide textual evidence from the novel to support interpretation of this key scene from Chapter 14.

Activity: "Section IV Log-In" **Page #:** 37
Focus: Plot, etc. **Learning Type:** Individual
Description: Complete "Crystal Ball" worksheets in order to predict future events in the novel. Then choose from several options to add to Interactive Novel Logs.

NAME(S): _____

ACTING HER AGE?

In this section of the novel, Opal interacts with many people. With a partner, consider how Opal acts around such characters as Otis, the Dewberry brothers, Gloria Dump, Miss Franny, and Amanda Wilkinson.

✦ In the left column, write any examples of when Opal's thoughts or actions are very mature (grown up) for her age.

✦ In the right column, write examples of when Opal's thoughts or actions are immature or inconsiderate.

Just use examples from Chapters 12–15.

Opal Acts Mature	Opal Acts Immature

With your partner, answer these questions.

1. What do the examples in the left column seem to have in common?

_____

_____

2. What do the examples in the right column seem to have in common?

_____

_____

3. What conclusions can you draw from your answers to #1 and #2? Be specific.

_____

_____

_____

NAME: _____

CHARACTER CLOSE-UPS

In this section of the novel, Opal gets to know a lot more about some of the characters she has recently met. Some of the information is about the characters' pasts or how they look or act. Some of what she learns is surprising.

Fill out the chart below and on page 35 to keep track of all the information Opal learned in these chapters.

	Otis	Gloria Dump
What new things does Opal learn about this character? Name at least two things.		
How does this new information explain this character's behavior or how other people view this character?		
How does this new information affect Opal's view or understanding of this character?		

CHARACTER CLOSE-UPS (CONT.)

	Sweetie Pie Thomas	Miss Franny	the Dewberry brothers
What does Opal learn about this character? Name at least one thing.			
How does this new information explain this character's behavior or how other people view this character?			
How does this new information affect Opal's view or understanding of this character?			

+ +

Considering Character

1. Of all the things Opal learns in this section about these six characters, which do you think is the most surprising to her? Explain.

   _____

   _____

   _____

2. Of all the things Opal learns in this section about these six characters, which do you think most makes her feel closer to the character? Explain.

   _____

   _____

   _____

   _____

NAME: _____

THE BIG OLD TREE

In Chapter 14, Gloria takes Opal further into her yard and shows her something unexpected. Answer the following questions. Provide quotations from the novel to support your answers.

1. Describe the "big old tree" in Gloria's yard. Write about where it is located and what it looks like.

   _____

   _____

   _____

   Quotation: _____

   _____ Page Number: _____

2. What does the tree symbolize to Gloria? In other words, what does it stand for?

   _____

   _____

   Quotation: _____

   _____ Page Number: _____

3. Why does Gloria share this tree with Opal? Why does she think it can serve as an important symbol for Opal, too?

   _____

   _____

   _____

   Quotation: _____

   _____ Page Number: _____

4. What connection does Opal make between the tree and her own past?

   _____

   _____

   _____

   Quotation: _____

   _____ Page Number: _____

SECTION IV LOG-IN

Now that you have finished the activities this section of *Because of Winn-Dixie*, take some time to add to your Interactive Novel Log before you begin reading the next section.

✦ **First, make a prediction about what will happen next in the novel.**
  Use your "Crystal Ball" worksheet (page 15) to do this.

✦ **Next, make a more personal connection to what you have read.**
  Choose one of the suggestions below and use it to fill a page in your Interactive Novel Log. Take this opportunity to connect with the novel in a way that appeals to you.

+ +

Ideas for Your Interactive Novel Log

1
Problem Solving

In the pet store, Opal and Otis frantically try to catch all the animals that are out of their cages. Then Opal gets an idea that makes the job much easier. Write about a time when you solved a problem with a good idea or witnessed someone else solve a problem.

2
Judging Others

When Gloria Dump shows Opal her bottle tree, she reminds Opal not to judge others too quickly. Was there a time when you judged someone too quickly and later learned something that changed your mind about that person? Write about a time when you did this or when you witnessed someone else do it.

3
Book Suggestion

Opal asks Miss Franny to suggest a book to read to Gloria Dump. If she had asked you, which book would you suggest? Why? Would you choose your favorite, or would you choose one that you think would appeal to a character like Gloria? Explain your answer.

4
Acrostic Poems

Use one or more character names to create an acrostic poem about the characters or events in the novel up until this point. Write the name of the character down the page. Then write one word for each letter that describes the character or something important about the story. You may also choose to do a poem for the town of Naomi. Try writing more than one poem.

N _____
A _____
O _____
M _____
I _____

TEACHER INSTRUCTIONS

In this section of *Because of Winn-Dixie*, Opal learns about Littmus Lozenges and shares them with her father and her new friends.

After your students have read Chapters 16–19, have them begin their analyses of this section of the novel by completing the following activities for their Interactive Novel Logs. Each of these activities is to be done individually.

✦ **"The Summaries of Its Parts"** (page 10)

✦ **"Major Minors"** (page 11)

✦ **"Because of the Title"** (page 12)

✦ **"Checking In on Theme"** (page 13)

✦ **"Choice Words"** (page 14)

> For this section, distribute new copies of the Interactive Novel Log worksheets on pages 10–14.

Students will then further examine this section through the following worksheets:

Activity: "The Story of the War"　　　　　　**Page #:** 39
Focus: Plot, Characterization　　　　　　**Learning Type:** Individual
Description: Examine the dynamic between the three characters (one teller and two listeners) involved in Miss Franny's story of Littmus W. Block.

Activity: "Encyclopedia Entry"　　　　　　**Page #:** 40
Focus: Plot　　　　　　**Learning Type:** Individual
Description: Create an entry about Littmus Lozenges for an online encyclopedia about candy. Use the information given in the novel to craft a realistic entry.

Activity: "A Taste of Sorrow"　　　　　　**Page #:** 41
Focus: Plot　　　　　　**Learning Type:** Individual
Description: Chart the reactions of each character to the Littmus Lozenge. Draw conclusions based on this information.

Activity: "Section V Log-In"　　　　　　**Page #:** 42
Focus: Plot, etc.　　　　　　**Learning Type:** Individual
Description: Complete "Crystal Ball" worksheets in order to predict future events in the novel. Then choose from several options to add to Interactive Novel Logs.

NAME: _____

THE STORY OF THE WAR

The first two chapters of this section are devoted to Miss Franny's story and how Opal and Amanda react to it.

1. When Miss Franny begins to tell her story, how do you think Opal feels about listening along with Amanda Wilkinson?

   _____

   _____

2. During which war does Miss Franny's story take place?

   _____

3. What reminded Miss Franny of this war and made her want to tell the story?

   _____

   _____

4. What does Miss Franny say is the event that started this war?

   _____

5. What are Miss Franny's views on war? Provide two quotations that show her feelings about it.

   a. _____

   _____

   b. _____

   _____

6. Compare and contrast Opal's reactions to the story to Amanda's reaction.

   a. How are their reactions and ways of listening to the story similar?

   _____

   _____

   b. How are their reactions and ways of listening to the story different?

   _____

   _____

7. As the story ends, does Opal still feel the same about Amanda being there? Explain.

   _____

   _____

NAME: _____

ENCYCLOPEDIA ENTRY

In Chapter 17, Miss Franny tells the story of Littmus Lozenges. Imagine you are asked to write an encyclopedia entry about Littmus Lozenges for a website called Candylandia.

Encyclopedia entries should not contain opinions. They should only report facts. For each section of your entry, include the following information:

✦ **History** — information about the creator of the candy and how he came to create them

✦ **Description** — information about packaging, flavor, etc.

✦ **Public Reaction** — information about the candy's past and current popularity and how people react to eating the candy

---

Welcome to Candylandia
an online encyclopedia for every candy imaginable

Littmus Lozenges

History

Description

Public Reaction

A TASTE OF SORROW

In this section of the novel, most of the characters try a Littmus Lozenge. Record their reactions in the chart below.

Character	What it made him/her think of or feel like
Amanda	
Gloria	
the Preacher	
Otis	
Sweetie Pie	

1. Name three reactions that Opal has to the candy. Put them in order of the most sorrowful to the least.

   Most Sorrowful ➔ 1. _____

   2. _____

   Least Sorrowful ➔ 3. _____

2. Whose reaction to the candy was most surprising to Opal? Why? What did she learn from this person's reaction?

   _____

   _____

   _____

3. Why do you think Opal wanted to share the candy with Gloria, Otis, and her father?

   _____

   _____

   _____

   _____

NAME: _____

SECTION V LOG-IN

Now that you have finished the activities for this section of *Because of Winn-Dixie*, take some time to add to your Interactive Novel Log before you begin reading the next section.

✦ **First, make a prediction about what will happen next in the novel.**

Use your "Crystal Ball" worksheet (page 15) to do this.

✦ **Next, make a more personal connection to what you have read.**

Choose one of the suggestions below and use it to fill a page in your Interactive Novel Log. Take this opportunity to connect with the novel in a way that appeals to you.

+ +

Ideas for Your Interactive Novel Log

1
The Firing on Fort Sumter

Do research to learn more about the firing on Fort Sumter. Devote a page to that event and its role in the U.S. Civil War.

2
One Great Great-Grandparent

Miss Franny tells the story of how her great-grandfather survived a war and started a company that created a family fortune. Do research to find out more about one of your great-grandparents. Where was he or she born? What did he or she do? What stories have been passed down about him or her?

3
Hidden Music

In Chapter 18, Opal says she likes the sound of the word *melancholy*. She feels like there is music hidden somewhere in it. Choose one word or make a list of words that you feel that way about. Decorate your page with these words and explain why you like the sound of them so much.

4
Candy Blog

Littmus Lozenges make people a little sad. Think of the candy that makes you the happiest when you are eating it. Use a page in your log to highlight this candy. Use drawings and descriptive language to tell readers why this candy is so amazing. Since this is a blog, you can focus on your opinion and you can write with personality.

TEACHER INSTRUCTIONS

In this section of *Because of Winn-Dixie*, Opal decides to plan a party, to which she invites all of her new friends. However, an unexpected event quickly changes the tone of the event.

After your students have read Chapters 20–23, have them begin their analyses of this section of the novel by completing the following activities for their Interactive Novel Logs. Each of these activities is to be done individually.

(**Note:** Do not distribute the "Major Minors" worksheet, as no new minor characters are introduced in this section.)

✦ **"The Summaries of Its Parts"** (page 10)

✦ **"Because of the Title"** (page 12)

✦ **"Checking In on Theme"** (page 13)

✦ **"Choice Words"** (page 14)

> For this section, distribute new copies of the Interactive Novel Log worksheets on pages 10, 12, 13, and 14.

✦ ✦

Students will then further examine this section through the following worksheets:

Activity: "Characteristic Reactions" **Page #:** 44-45
Focus: Characterization **Learning Type:** Individual
Description: Record each character's reaction to Opal's party invitation. Determine what these reactions say about the personalities of these characters.

Activity: "Conflicting Feelings" **Page #:** 46
Focus: Plot, Craft and Structure **Learning Type:** Individual
Description: Examine the author's introduction of conflict at the end of Chapter 23. Consider its place in the novel as a whole and its effect on the reader.

Activity: "Was This Foreshadowed?" **Page #:** 47
Focus: Plot, Craft and Structure **Learning Type:** Individual
Description: Think about earlier events in the novel and how they might have provided clues to events that occur in this section.

Activity: "Words of Wisdom" **Page #:** 48
Focus: Plot, Theme **Learning Type:** Collaborative
Description: Practice speaking and listening skills by discussing quotes given in this section and determining how they fit in with themes established in the novel.

Activity: "Section VI Log-In" **Page #:** 49
Focus: Plot, etc. **Learning Type:** Individual
Description: Complete "Crystal Ball" worksheets in order to predict future events in the novel. Then choose from several options to add to Interactive Novel Logs.

CHARACTERISTIC REACTIONS

In Chapter 20, Opal decides that she and Gloria will throw a party and invite all of her new friends. Take note of the reactions of each character. What do those reactions say about those characters?

For each character listed below, tell what his or her reaction was to the news of Opal's party. Then explain what you think this reaction says about the character.

	How does this character react to Opal's invitation?	What does this reaction say about this character? Explain.
Gloria Dump		
the Preacher		
Miss Franny Block		
Amanda Wilkinson		
Sweetie Pie Thomas		

44

NAME: _____

Chapters 20–23

CHARACTERISTIC REACTIONS (CONT.)

	How does this character react?	What does this reaction say about this character? Explain.
Stevie Dewberry		
Dunlap Dewberry		
Otis		

+ +

Considering Characterization

1. Did any character's reaction surprise you? Explain._____

_____

_____

_____

2. Which character's reaction was the most like your reaction would be to an invitation to Opal's party? Explain.

_____

_____

_____

_____

©Teacher Created Resources   45   #8200 In-Depth Guide to Because of Winn-Dixie

NAME: _____

CONFLICTING FEELINGS

In literature, a **conflict** is a struggle between opposing forces. A conflict can be between two people, or it can be a struggle that takes place within one character. A conflict can also be with nature or society. The way a conflict is introduced (begins), evolves (changes), and then resolves (ends) is often what lends excitement and interest to a novel.

1. What is the main conflict that is introduced near the end of Chapter 23?

    _____

    _____

2. How is this conflict similar to other conflicts in the novel?

    _____

    _____

    _____

3. How is it different from other conflicts in the novel?

    _____

    _____

    _____

4. In your opinion, is this the biggest conflict that Opal has faced so far in this novel?

    ❏ **YES**   ❏ **NO**

    Explain your answer. _____

    _____

    _____

5. What do you think the author is trying to make you feel as you read this part?

    _____

    _____

6. Was the author successful in making you feel this way? Explain your answer.

    _____

    _____

    _____

    _____

NAME: _____

WAS THIS FORESHADOWED?

In literature, **foreshadowing** is a device authors use to give readers clues about a plot turn or twist that will occur later in the novel. Consider the ending of Chapter 23 and decide if it was foreshadowed by earlier events.

1. What have we learned previously in the book about thunderstorms in the summer in Florida?

    _____

    _____

2. From whom did we learn this information?

    _____

3. What was happening in the novel when we learned this information?

    _____

    _____

4. How does that earlier event foreshadow what happens at Opal's party?

    _____

    _____

    _____

    _____

5. Who first notices that Winn-Dixie is missing?

    _____

6. When the thunderstorm interrupts the party, why do you think Opal loses track of Winn-Dixie?

    _____

    _____

    _____

7. Did you as a reader also lose track of Winn-Dixie? Did you forget about her pathological fear? If so, why do you think you did?

    _____

    _____

    _____

NAME(S): _____

WORDS OF WISDOM

In this section, Gloria gives Opal some advice and offers her views on the world. With a partner, discuss Gloria's words and how they fit in with the themes and events of the novel. Begin by deciding who will be Speaker #1 and who will be Speaker #2.

Speaker #1's Name: _____ **Speaker #2's Name:** _____

Speaker #1

Think about the following quote from Gloria Dump: *"I believe, sometimes, that the whole world has an aching heart."*

✦ Tell your partner how this quote fits in with this scene from the novel and also with the novel as a whole. Which characters or situations from the novel show the meaning of this quote?

Speaker #2

✦ Listen to your partner's words. Tell him or her if you agree or disagree with them, and explain your opinion.

✦ Add any information that you feel your partner left out when answering this question.

Now switch roles.

Speaker #2

Think about the following quote from Gloria Dump: *"There ain't no way you can hold onto something that wants to go."*

✦ Tell your partner how this quote fits in with this scene from the novel and also with the novel as a whole. Which characters or situations from the novel show the meaning of this quote?

Speaker #1

✦ Listen to your partner's words. Tell him or her if you agree or disagree with them, and explain your opinion.

✦ Add any information that you feel your partner left out when answering this question.

Next, work together.

After you have discussed Gloria's words, talk about this quote from Sweetie Pie Thomas: "That dog ain't lost. That dog's too smart to get lost." Do you agree with what Sweetie Pie says? As a group, give your answer and explain it.

SECTION VI LOG-IN

Now that you have finished the activities for this section of *Because of Winn-Dixie*, take some time to add to your Interactive Novel Log before you begin reading the next section.

✦ **First, make a prediction about what will happen next in the novel.**

Use your "Crystal Ball" worksheet (page 15) to do this.

✦ **Next, make a more personal connection to what you have read.**

Choose one of the suggestions below and use it to fill a page in your Interactive Novel Log. Take this opportunity to connect with the novel in a way that appeals to you.

Ideas for Your Interactive Novel Log

1
Character Invites

Imagine you could throw a party to which you can invite 6-8 fictional characters. Which characters would you choose to invite? Write the name of each character, along with an explanation of why that character would make a good (or interesting) party guest.

2
Dump Punch

For the party, Gloria makes her "world famous" Dump Punch. Create a recipe for a party punch named after you. Design a magazine article about your famous beverage. It should include the list of ingredients, a picture of your drink, and a few quotes from you about what makes your punch so special.

3
Set the Scene

Without rereading the section, draw a picture of the party scene right before the rains come. Include details about the characters, such as what they are wearing, what they brought with them, etc. Under your picture, write the three details about the party that you remember most vividly.

4
Ruined by Rain

Have you ever had an event in your life ruined by the weather? Write about a time when plans you had made were changed by weather that was too wet, too cold, or too hot. What happened as a result?

TEACHER INSTRUCTIONS

In this section of *Because of Winn-Dixie*, Opal thinks she has lost Winn-Dixie forever, only to find out that her beloved pet didn't run away after all.

After your students have read Chapters 24–26, have them begin their analyses of this section of the novel by completing the following activities for their Interactive Novel Logs. Each of these activities is to be done individually.

(**Note:** Do not distribute the "Major Minors" worksheet, as no new minor characters are introduced in this section.)

✦ **"The Summaries of Its Parts"** (page 10)

✦ **"Because of the Title"** (page 12)

✦ **"Checking In on Theme"** (page 13)

✦ **"Choice Words"** (page 14)

> For this section, distribute new copies of the Interactive Novel Log worksheets on pages 10, 12, 13, and 14.

+ +

Students will then further examine this section through the following worksheets:

Activity: "Two Timelines" **Page #:** 51
Focus: Plot **Learning Type:** Individual
Description: Organize the events of this last section of the book by charting the separate experiences of each group of characters: the one that stayed at the party and the one that went looking for Winn-Dixie.

Activity: "Acting Out" **Page #:** 52–53
Focus: Plot, Characterization **Learning Type:** Collaborative
Description: Work within a large group to dramatize the party scene after Opal leaves to find her dog. (**TIP:** Divide the class into groups of 5–8 students. Not all roles listed on page 52 need to be assigned to each group.)

Activity: "The End of the Story" **Page #:** 54
Focus: Plot **Learning Type:** Individual
Description: Reflect on the ending of the novel, and consider how an alternate ending might have affected a reader's impressions of the novel as a whole.

Activity: "Section VII Log-In" **Page #:** 55
Focus: Plot, etc. **Learning Type:** Individual
Description: Complete "Crystal Ball" worksheets in order to predict future events in the novel. Then choose from several options to add to Interactive Novel Logs.

NAME: _____

TWO TIMELINES

This section begins with Opal and her father leaving the party to search for Winn-Dixie. Meanwhile, many other characters are still gathered at Gloria's house.

Use the diagrams below to create two timelines for each of these groups of people. Begin by naming the charactors involved in each group.

Group 1 Characters: _____

Where They Were: _____ on the streets of Naomi _____

On the diagram, list four experiences this group had during this part of the story. Put the experiences in the order they happened.

1.	3.

2.	4.

Group 2 Characters: _____

Where They Were: _____ in Gloria Dump's house _____

On the diagram, list four experiences this group had during this part of the story. Put the experiences in the order they happened.

1.	3.

2.	4.

NAME(S): _____

ACTING OUT

Because of Winn-Dixie is told from Opal's perspective. As readers, we are only able to witness what Opal witnesses. As a result, we don't get to see or hear what goes on at Gloria's house once Opal leaves. When Opal returns, the other characters tell her what happened, but they only give her a few details.

Your group will recreate the party scene once Opal leaves. Together, you will write a script that dramatizes this scene. You will use the information given in the novel to imagine what the characters said and did from the time Opal left until the time she returned. Make up dialogue and act out your scene for the class.

Use the information below and on page 53 to plan out your scene. Then write your scene on a separate piece of paper.

+ +

Cast (the characters in the scene)

Include as many characters as possible, but not all need by portrayed.

Who are the characters in this scene?	Who will play each character?
Gloria Dump	
Miss Franny Block	
Otis	
Amanda Wilkinson	
Dunlap Dewberry	
Stevie Dewberry	
Sweetie Pie Thomas	
Gertrude	

Props (the objects in the scene)

Props Needed	Why?

ACTING OUT (CONT.)

Dialogue (the words spoken in the scene)

Important Lines of Dialogue to Include

✛ ✛

Tips for Writing a Script

Your script should contain these three elements:

✦ **Character Names** — The name of the characters in the scene should be written in the script. *Each time a character's name appears, it should be written in uppercase letters. Each time the character speaks, his or her name should be centered over his or her words.*

✦ **Dialogue** — Dialogue is what the characters say. Most of your script will be dialogue. You do not need to put quotation marks around dialogue in your script. *Center each line of dialogue under the name of the character who is speaking.*

✦ **Stage Directions** — This information describes what the characters should be doing in the scene or other things that are happening besides dialogue. This information helps the actors know what to do. These sentences are not read or spoken out loud. Instead, the audience sees the actors perform these actions. *Put these sentences in parentheses.*

NAME: _____

THE END OF THE STORY

The ending of a book should follow logically from the sequence of events in the story. Use the questions below to examine the ending of *Because of Winn-Dixie*.

1. How does the novel end? Summarize the events.

   _____

   _____

   _____

   _____

   _____

2. Did it end the way you expected it to? Explain.

   _____

   _____

3. Do you feel that this ending fits the story? Explain.

   _____

   _____

   _____

   _____

4. How would you feel if the novel had ended differently? Imagine that the novel had ended with Opal not finding Winn-Dixie but still having her new friends there to support her through the difficulty of that loss. How would this have affected your feelings about the book? Write a paragraph in which you explain your thoughts on this subject.

   _____

   _____

   _____

   _____

   _____

   _____

   _____

SECTION VII LOG-IN

Now that you have finished reading the novel, take some time to add to your Interactive Novel Log.

- ✦ **First, make a prediction about what will happen next in the lives of some of this novel's characters.**

  Use your "Crystal Ball" worksheet (page 15) to do this.

- ✦ **Next, make a more personal connection to what you have read.**

  Choose one of the suggestions below and use it to fill a page in your Interactive Novel Log. Take this opportunity to connect with the novel in a way that appeals to you.

✦ ✦

Ideas for Your Interactive Novel Log

1
In a Word

Think about how you would complete this sentence: *This book makes me think about* _____. Write this word in the middle of a page. Fill the rest of the page with pictures, words, and quotations that relate to this word.

2
Fantastic Finishes

What book or movie has your favorite ending? Name the book or movie, describe why you like the ending so much, and compare its ending to that of *Because of Winn-Dixie*.

3
Reset the Setting

Imagine that you are Opal, and you are searching for Winn-Dixie in your city or town. Draw a map of your town, and show the route you would walk as you search for Winn-Dixie. Next to each location, state why you would look for Winn-Dixie there.

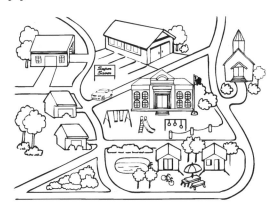

4
Movie Review

A movie version of *Because of Winn-Dixie* was released in 2005. Have you seen it? If so, how did it compare to the book? If you haven't, would you like to? Why or why not?

TEACHER INSTRUCTIONS

After your students have finished reading *Because of Winn-Dixie*, they can further their in-depth analysis of the novel through the use of the following worksheets:

✦ ✦

Activity: "Add It Up"　　　　**Page #:** 57–59　　　　**Learning Type:** Individual
Description: Use the work done in the Interactive Novel Logs to sum up thoughts on the novel as a whole.

Activity: "All About Opal"　　　　**Page #:** 60　　　　**Learning Type:** Individual
Description: Make a list of 10 things about the main character of the novel. Analyze an idea from the novel and decide on the ways in which it can and cannot be applied to your list.

Activity: "Letter to Mama"　　　　**Page #:** 61　　　　**Learning Type:** Individual
Description: Practice writing in the voice of the novel's narrator. Write a letter that focuses on one memorable event from the story. (**TIP:** Read aloud select letters, focusing on how well students captured Opal's narrative voice.)

Activity: "A New Point of View"　　　　**Page #:** 62　　　　**Learning Type:** Individual
Description: Rewrite a scene in the novel from a third-person perspective. Think about how point of view affects story.

Activity: "Considering Genre"　　　　**Page #:** 63　　　　**Learning Type:** Individual
Description: Give reasons why the novel could fit into more than one genre. Rewrite a scene from the novel in an entirely different genre.

Activity: "Interview a Character"　　　　**Page #:** 64–65　　　　**Learning Type:** Collaborative
Description: In pairs, role-play as a character and an interviewer in front of the class. Utilize the tips provided on page 65.

Activity: "A Novel Poster"　　　　**Page #:** 66–67　　　　**Learning Type:** Collaborative
Description: Collaborate to create a poster that identifies key points in a chapter and shows understanding of the elements that contribute to that chapter's success. (**TIP:** Follow the detailed teacher instructions provided on page 66.)

Activity: "An Elemental Choice"　　　　**Page #:** 68–69　　　　**Learning Type:** Individual
Description: Plan and write a persuasive essay on which element *most* makes the novel special: voice, plot, or theme. Complete the outline form and use the two checklists to hone essays prior to writing a final draft.

Activity: "A Tale of Two Summers"　　　　**Page #:** 70–71　　　　**Learning Type:** Individual
Description: Plan and write a comparison essay based on Opal's experiences during the summer in Naomi, Florida. (**TIP:** For this activity, have students refer back to their "Summer in Your Town" worksheets from page 9.)

Activity: "A Persuasive Letter"　　　　**Page #:** 72　　　　**Learning Type:** Individual
Description: Use a letter-writing format to construct an argument and support that opinion with evidence from the text.

Activity: "My Book Rating"　　　　**Page #:** 73　　　　**Learning Type:** Individual
Description: Use a rating system to evaluate different components of the story before making a final evaluation of the book as a whole.

ADD IT UP

A novel is the sum of its parts. It is a combination of the events (plot) and people (characters) it describes. Look back at the work you have done for each section of *Because of Winn-Dixie*. Decide how the parts add up to form the novel as a whole.

The Summaries of Its Parts

Now that you have finished the novel — and have had a lot of practice with summarization — use your skills to write a very brief summary of the entire novel. Fit your statement on the lines below. To do so, you must include only the most important events in your summary.

_____

_____

_____

_____

_____

_____

_____

_____

_____

Now your teacher will read you the Book Summary included in the teacher guide (page 7). Listen closely and answer the following questions.

1. Is there anything you felt this summary should have included but didn't? Explain.

_____

_____

2. Does this summary give someone who hasn't read the book a good idea of what to expect? Explain.

_____

_____

3. Would you say that this book is easy or challenging to summarize? Explain.

_____

_____

NAME: _____

ADD IT UP (CONT.)

Major Minors

1. Of all the minor characters introduced in this novel, which one do you think is most important to the story?

[ ]

Explain your answer. _____

_____

_____

_____

2. How would the novel have been different without this character?

_____

_____

_____

_____

Because of the Title

1. Of all the events that happen because of Winn-Dixie, which event is the most important for Opal?

_____

_____

2. Explain why you chose this event and how it changed things for Opal.

_____

_____

_____

_____

_____

_____

NAME: _____

ADD IT UP (CONT.)

1. Of all the themes introduced in this novel, which is the most important theme? Check off one box below.

   ❑ **Abandonment** (being left behind by someone or something)

   ❑ **Acceptance** (learning to accept people for who they are)

   ❑ **Communication** (understanding others and being understood)

   ❑ **Courage** (being strong enough to be yourself and to move forward)

   ❑ **Friendship** (forming bonds with other people or animals)

   ❑ **Loneliness** (feeling alone in the world)

   ❑ **Other** (Is the most important theme not listed? Name it here.) _____

2. Explain your choice here. _____

   _____

   _____

   _____

   _____

   _____

Crystal Ball

Look back at your predictions for each section of *Because of Winn-Dixie*.

1. Which of your predictions came true just like you thought they would?

   _____

   _____

   _____

2. Which of your predictions were very different from what ended up happening?

   _____

   _____

   _____

NAME: _____

ALL ABOUT OPAL

Early in the novel, Opal asks her father to name 10 things about her mama. Imagine that Opal's mama calls the Preacher one day and wants to know 10 things about Opal. What should he tell her? Make a list of the 10 most important things to know about Opal.

Things to Know About India Opal Buloni

1. _____
2. _____
3. _____
4. _____
5. _____
6. _____
7. _____
8. _____
9. _____
10. _____

Near the end of the novel, Opal realizes that knowing 10 things about a person doesn't really help you get to know the real person. See if you agree with that.

✦ Why would your list of 10 things really help someone know who Opal is?

_____

_____

_____

_____

✦ Why would your list not be enough to help someone really know who Opal is?

_____

_____

_____

_____

NAME: _____

LETTER TO MAMA

Throughout the novel, Opal experiences events and wishes she could tell her mama about them. Use a letter format to write about one of these events. Write your letter to Opal's mama. Opal is the narrator of *Because of Winn-Dixie*. Think about her voice—the way she thinks and talks. Try to use Opal's voice in your letter.

Choose one of the following scenes to write about:

❑ Opal meets Winn-Dixie
❑ Winn-Dixie catches the mouse in church
❑ Miss Franny tells the story of the bear
❑ Opal meets Gloria Dump
❑ Opal gets a job at the pet store

❑ the thunderstorm in the middle of the night
❑ Opal's friends try Littmus Lozenges
❑ Opal plans a party

Dear Mama,

_____
_____
_____
_____
_____
_____
_____
_____
_____
_____
_____
_____
_____
_____
_____
_____
_____

NAME: _____

A NEW POINT OF VIEW

Because of Winn-Dixie is written in first-person point of view. This means that the author uses pronouns such as "I" and "me" when writing about Opal's experiences. It also means that we the readers can only experience what Opal experiences. We can't know what other people are thinking or what they're doing when Opal is not around. When a novel is written in third-person point of view, the author uses pronouns such as "she" and "her." In third-person narration, we can know what each character is thinking.

Choose an important scene from the novel, such as one when Opal meets one of her new friends in town. Rewrite a few paragraphs from that scene. This time, however, use the third-person point of view to show what happens during the scene.

_____

_____

_____

_____

_____

_____

_____

_____

_____

_____

_____

_____

_____

_____

+ +

Considering Craft

1. How do you think the novel would have changed if the author had used the third-person point of view?

_____

_____

2. Why do you think the author chose to use first-person perspective in this novel?

_____

_____

_____

NAME: _____

CONSIDERING GENRE

In literature, the word *genre* refers to the category into which a novel fits. Some examples of genres are historical fiction, science fiction, fantasy, and contemporary fiction. Books that fit into a certain genre usually share similar form, style, or subject matter.

Because of Winn-Dixie mostly takes place in the real world and has familiar people and places. This would put it in the genre of **realistic fiction.** However, the novel also has a few elements of magic in it, which could make it a part of the genre known as **magic realism**.

List elements of the story that seem very realistic: _____

_____

_____

List an element or two that seem more magical: _____

_____

_____

Imagine if *Because of Winn-Dixie* had been written in a completely different genre. Choose and circle one of the genres below. Then rewrite a short scene from *Because of Winn-Dixie*, but change the action so that it best fits into this new genre. Use a separate piece of paper if more room is needed.

adventure	fable	fantasy	science fiction

_____

_____

_____

_____

_____

_____

_____

_____

_____

_____

INTERVIEW A CHARACTER

Opal is the main character in *Because of Winn-Dixie*, but the other characters are important, too. The secondary characters help readers understand the main character better and help move the plot along. You and a partner will analyze one secondary character and create a mock interview that demonstrates the character's personality.

Your teacher will assign one of these secondary characters to you and your partner:

- ❑ the Preacher
- ❑ Amanda Wilkinson
- ❑ Dunlap Dewberry
- ❑ Gloria Dump
- ❑ Sweetie Pie Thomas
- ❑ Stevie Dewberry
- ❑ Miss Franny Block
- ❑ Otis

> **Once you have been assigned a character, write his or her name here:**
>
> _____

You and your partner will present a live interview of your assigned character. One of you will pretend to be the character, while the other will be the interviewer. Work together to plan your interview. Write five questions you would like to ask your assigned character. Use questions that require more than a one-word answer. In order to do this, use question starters such as the following:

1. Tell us about _____

_____

2. What did you think when _____

_____

3. How would you _____

_____

4. Explain why _____

_____

Now come up with a question of your own.

5. _____

_____

NAME(S): _____

INTERVIEW A CHARACTER (CONT.)
MAKINGS OF A GREAT INTERVIEW

You and your partner will be conducting an interview in front of the class, so you both will want to make it great. First and foremost, you will want to be prepared.

+ Discuss the types of questions the interviewer will be asking.

+ Discuss how the character would answer these questions.

+ Practice your presentation!

In addition, each member of the team can use a few helpful tips to make the interview a success.

Interviewer

❑ Before the actual presentation, prepare note cards with brief hints that will help you remember your opening statement, the questions you will be asking, etc.

❑ Begin by giving the audience a brief introduction to the character.

❑ Explain how the character knows Opal.

❑ Provide an interesting fact about the character.

❑ Ask at least four questions. Remember to make your questions ones that require more than a one-word answer.

❑ Be sure to listen to the interviewee's responses and wait until your partner is finished speaking before moving on to the next question.

❑ Conclude the interview by asking the audience if they have any questions for the character.

Interviewee

❑ Pretend that you are the character throughout the interview.

❑ Answer the questions as you imagine the character would answer them.

❑ If possible, try to talk and act the way you imagine the character would.

❑ Listen to the interviewer carefully and wait until he or she is finished asking each question before responding.

A Novel Poster
Teacher Instructions

This activity offers students an opportunity to demonstrate understanding of the novel by creating visual representations of its parts.

Materials Required: poster board, markers

Optional Materials: scissors, glue, magazines, Internet access, sticky notes

- ✦ To begin, divide the class into groups of students. The ideal number in each group is 4, but smaller or larger groups will also be possible.
- ✦ Next, assign a chapter from the novel to each group. Choose from the chapters listed on the student page.
- ✦ Distribute the second page of this activity. Have students read the instructions for what to include on their posters.
- ✦ Give students plenty of time to plan and create their posters. If you wish, allow them to access magazines or the Internet in search of appropriate images to include.
- ✦ After groups have completed their posters, hang the posters around the room. Conduct a gallery walk.

Ideas for a Gallery Walk

Allow students to move around the room and examine each poster. Equip students with sticky notes. When they have questions regarding other groups' posters, they may write their questions on sticky notes and attach these notes directly to the posters. Guide your students to ask questions such as the following:

- ✦ Is an idea on the poster not clear?
- ✦ Do you disagree with a point the poster makes?
- ✦ Do you want more information about something the group has included?
- ✦ Do you want to ask how the group felt about any particular scene or character?
- ✦ Do you want to bring up something you thought was important in that chapter but isn't included on the poster?

Once students have completed this process, allow groups to answer the questions attached to their posters.

A NOVEL POSTER

Your group will work together to create a poster that represents one chapter from *Because of Winn-Dixie*. Your teacher will assign your group one of the following chapters.

Chapter 1	**Chapter 9**	**Chapter 20**
Chapter 5	**Chapter 11**	**Chapter 23**
Chapter 8	**Chapter 12**	**Chapter 26**

Our group has been assigned Chapter _____.

First, your group should discuss the events in your section and decide which details are the most important.

Your poster should contain the following elements. Decide who will be in charge of each.

	Elements	Assigned to
1	• the number of the chapter • a short explanation of what happens in this chapter	
2	• a quotation from this chapter • a short explanation of the significance of the quotation	
3	• a picture representing the most important event in this chapter • a short description of the event	
4	• a picture that represents the setting of this event • a one-sentence explanation of where the event takes place	

Tips for Making Posters

✦ **Be creative!** You may draw pictures, use pictures from magazines, print images from the Internet (with permission from your teacher), or paste on objects that relate to the story.

✦ **Plan before you start.** Everyone should collect pictures and ideas before anyone begins writing on the poster board. Work together to design the look of the poster by placing all pictures before you paste them. Don't forget to leave room for the written parts.

NAME: _____

AN ELEMENTAL CHOICE

Because of Winn-Dixie is narrated by Opal. She and the other characters in the novel experience many events. These events help Opal and the other characters learn and grow.

In literature, three of the terms that we can discuss are **voice**, **plot**, and **theme**.

Voice	Plot	Theme
the speech and thought patterns of the first–person narrator	the events that take place in the novel	the underlying idea(s) or message(s) in the novel

Write an essay in which you argue that one of these elements is the most important part of the novel. Do you think that what makes this novel the most special is the voice of its narrator, the events she describes, or the ideas about life that author has included?

✦ ✦

Follow this outline to brainstorm ideas and to plan your rough draft.

Paragraph 1: Set up your essay by introducing the three terms and giving a brief description of how each element is used in the novel.

How **Voice** is used: _____

_____

How **Plot** is used: _____

_____

How **Theme** is used: _____

_____

Finish this first paragraph by stating which element you feel most makes the novel unique, interesting, or entertaining.

Paragraph 2: Use this paragraph to support the claim you made at the end of Paragraph 1. Give three examples that show how this element contributes to the success of the novel.

Example 1: _____

Example 2: _____

Example 3: _____

Paragraph 3: Restate your opinion and wrap up your essay.

After you have completed this outline, write a rough draft of your essay on a separate piece of paper. Use the checklists on the next page to make sure you have included all of the ingredients needed for a successful essay.

AN ELEMENTAL CHOICE (CONT.)

SELF-EDITING CHECKLIST

After writing your rough draft, use this checklist to make sure your essay has everything that is required. Check off the box next to each item once you have included that element in your essay.

- ☐ I have introduced the terms *voice*, *plot*, and *theme*.
- ☐ I have stated why each element is important to the novel.
- ☐ I have stated which element is most responsible for making the novel successful.
- ☐ I have given at least three examples that support my opinion.
- ☐ I have restated my opinion and concluded my essay.
- ☐ Throughout my essay, I used transition words to move from one example or paragraph to the next.
- ☐ I have checked my essay for spelling, punctuation, and grammar mistakes.

One thing I like about my essay is	One thing I need help with is

PEER-EDITING CHECKLIST

Have your partner read your essay, check a box for each statement, and respond to the questions below.

Reader's Name: _____	**Yes**	**No**
• The purpose of the essay is clearly stated and introduced.	☐	☐
• An opinion about the concept is clearly stated.	☐	☐
• Several examples and results of the family's struggles are given.	☐	☐
• Evidence from the novel is used to support claims.	☐	☐
• There are no spelling or grammar errors.	☐	☐

Did the writer give good examples that supported his or her claim? Explain.

_____

_____

_____

A TALE OF TWO SUMMERS

Before you began reading *Because of Winn-Dixie*, you completed a worksheet about summertime in your town. Now that you have read the novel, compare and contrast your summer with those of Opal and the other inhabitants of Naomi, Florida.

Your assignment is to write an essay in which you find similarities (compare) and differences (contrast) between your experience as a child in your town and those of Opal and the other child characters in *Because of Winn-Dixie*.

✦ ✦

Follow this outline in writing your essay. Use the space provided to brainstorm ideas and to plan your rough draft.

Paragraph 1: Introduce the concept of your essay. State what it will be about.

_____

_____

Paragraph 2: Use this paragraph to state the similarities between your summer experiences and those of the child characters (Opal, Sweetie Pie, Amanda, the Dewberry brothers) in the novel. Give two examples from the novel.

Example 1: _____

_____

Example 2: _____

_____

Paragraph 3: State the differences between your summer experiences and those of the child characters in the novel. Give two examples from the novel.

Example 1: _____

_____

Example 2: _____

_____

Paragraph 4: Conclude your essay by stating whether your summer experience is more similar or more different to those of the characters from the novel.

_____

_____

After you have completed this outline, write a rough draft of your essay on a separate piece of paper. Use the checklists on the next page to make sure you have included all of the ingredients needed for a successful essay.

NAME: _____

A TALE OF TWO SUMMERS (CONT.)

SELF-EDITING CHECKLIST

After writing your rough draft, use this checklist to make sure your essay has everything that is required. Check off the box next to each item once you have included that element in your essay.

- ☐ I have introduced the concept of the essay.
- ☐ I have focused on similarities and given two examples from the novel.
- ☐ I have focused on differences and given two examples from the novel.
- ☐ Throughout my essay, I used transition words to move from one example or paragraph to the next.
- ☐ I have checked my essay for spelling, punctuation, and grammar mistakes.

One thing I like about my essay is	One thing I need help with is

PEER-EDITING CHECKLIST

Have your partner read your essay, check a box for each statement, and respond to the questions below.

Reader's Name: _____	Yes	No
• The purpose of the essay is clearly stated and introduced.	☐	☐
• Two examples of the similarities are provided.	☐	☐
• Two examples of the differences are provided.	☐	☐
• There are no spelling or grammar errors.	☐	☐

Did the writer give good examples to show the similarities and differences? Explain.

_____

_____

_____

_____

NAME: _____

A PERSUASIVE LETTER

Imagine that another school is considering using *Because of Winn-Dixie* in its classrooms. First, they want your thoughts on the novel.

Write a letter to the principal of this imaginary school. Give your opinion of the book and explain why it should be taught there or why it should not.

Follow this outline, and then write your letter on a separate piece of paper.

Dear Principal,

Paragraph 1 should include this information:

➤ *the title of the book*
➤ *why and when you read this book*
➤ *your opinion of the book*
➤ *if other classes should read this book*

Paragraph 1 goes here.

Paragraph 2 should include this information:

➤ *one thing you liked or did not like about the book and why*
➤ *an example from the book*

Paragraph 2 goes here.

Paragraph 3 should include this information:

➤ *a second thing you liked or did not like about the book and why*
➤ *an example from the book*

Paragraph 3 goes here.

Concluding Sentence:

➤ *one sentence saying what you think the school should do*

Conclusion goes here.

Sincerely,

sign name——➤ *Your signature*

print name——➤ **Your name**

MY BOOK RATING

What did you like or dislike about the book? Think about the story elements and rank each one. Use the following rating scale.

0 stars	1 star	2 stars	3 stars	4 stars	5 stars
☆☆☆☆☆	★☆☆☆☆	★★☆☆☆	★★★☆☆	★★★★☆	★★★★★
terrible	bad	okay	good	great	amazing!

Characters ☆☆☆☆☆

Reason: _____

Setting ☆☆☆☆☆

Reason: _____

Point of View ☆☆☆☆☆

Reason: _____

Plot ☆☆☆☆☆

Reason: _____

The Ending ☆☆☆☆☆

Reason: _____

Theme ☆☆☆☆☆

Reason: _____

Overall, I give this book _____ stars because _____

_____

_____

TEACHER INSTRUCTIONS

Because of Winn-Dixie contains vocabulary that is integral to the novel's setting, characters, and themes. DiCamillo chooses to use many words that provide a vivid impression of the small town of Naomi and the situations in which the characters find themselves.

On page 75 is a list of the most challenging and important vocabulary words found in *Because of Winn-Dixie*. These words are listed in the order in which they appear in the novel. The chapter in which the word can be found is listed in parentheses after each word.

Select words from these section lists to assign for the "Choice Words" Interactive Novel Log entries (see page 14).

Other Ideas for Assigning Vocabulary

✦ **Traditional Vocabulary Lesson** — Select a total of 10 to 20 words for the entire class to study and learn.

✦ **Personalized Vocabulary** — Post the lists in the classroom and allow students to select their own word or words to study.

✦ **Students as Teachers** — For each section, assign a different word to pairs or groups of students and have them do short presentations on the word's meaning and use to the rest of the class.

After your students have finished reading the entire novel, review vocabulary from each section by using one or more of the following activities:

✦ **Create a crossword puzzle.** Use one vocabulary word from each section.

✦ **Write a poem.** Use one vocabulary word from each section.

✦ **Play a Jeopardy-style game.** Make a game board with definitions of the vocabulary words. Students or student groups compete to identify the correct words.

This adjective means "joyless" or "sorrowful."

What is **melancholy**?

✦ **Hold a vocabulary-in-context contest!** Have students write short stories that properly use as many vocabulary words as they can. Select a few stories with the highest number of vocabulary words used, read them aloud to the class, and have the class vote for the story that made the best use of vocabulary words.

Words to Know

NOVEL VOCABULARY

For each word, the chapter number is given in parentheses. The words can be found in the novel in the order in which they are shown here.

Section I	Section II	Section III	Section IV
employees (1)	motto (5)	installment (8)	slithering (12)
concern (1)	congregation (5)	mumbled (8)	criminal (12)
belong (1)	potluck (5)	drooped (8)	charming (12)
missionary (2)	skidding (5)	identical (9)	arranging (13)
exception (2)	selected (6)	general (9)	ignorant (13)
specifically (2)	positive (6)	whimpering (11)	roundabout (13)
fortunate (2)	trembling (6)	barreling (11)	imitated (14)
matted (2)	embarrassed (6)	pathological (11)	clanking (14)
muttering (3)	snuffled (6)	reasoned (11)	chattering (15)
nudge (3)	properly (6)	terrorized (11)	dramatic (15)
	peculiar (7)		

Section V	Section VI	Section VII
occurred (16)	aching (20)	memorized (24)
enlisted (16)	theme (20)	snuffly (24)
abiding (16)	swollen (21)	nerve (24)
convince (16)	desperately (21)	possible (25)
vermin (16)	shimmery (21)	sigh (25)
manufactured (17)	swayed (21)	creeping (25)
hunching (18)	shuffled (22)	constellations (26)
melancholy (18)	appreciate (22)	echoed (26)
idle (18)	rumble (22)	strummed (26)
squawked (19)	teetery (23)	blooming (26)

ANSWER KEY

For many of the questions in this resource, answers will vary and will be subject to interpretation. Accept student work that responds appropriately to the questions asked and provides evidence from the text when called for. Refer to the answers listed below when more specific responses may be needed.

✦ ✦

A Turtle in Its Shell (page 19)

2. He likes to hide inside his shell and only poke his head out when it's safe to do so.

4. She is comparing her father to a turtle, an animal he in most ways is very unlike.

Infer the Information (page 24)

1. She makes a comment about how large Winn-Dixie is, and she gives the dog a pat on his head.

2. Winn-Dixie shows her his teeth. He smiles at her.

3. She smiles back. His smile seem to make her perk up and not feel so alone.

4. Amanda tells Miss Franny that she has finished reading her book and would like a new one that is more difficult because she is an advanced reader.

5. Miss Franny responds, "Yes, dear, I know."

So to Speak (page 28)

Inside the Pet Store:

1. Opal and Otis

2. It's mostly about paying for the new collar and leash for Winn-Dixie.

3. Opal

Outside the Pet Store:

1. Opal and Sweetie Pie Thomas

2. It's mostly about things that Sweetie Pie has seen Winn-Dixie do.

3. Sweetie Pie Thomas

How You Know (page 29)

1. the first paragraph

2. They think she is a mean, old witch.

3. Yes, they know she is the preacher's daughter.

4. Winn-Dixie has jumped the fence and ran inside the yard.

What the Storm Brings (page 30)

1. A bad thunderstorm happens in the middle of the night.

2. Winn-Dixie is scared and frantic. He beats his head against the door and then runs around the house.

3. She stares in disbelief. She keeps out of his way.

4. He figures out that Winn-Dixie must have a pathological fear of thunderstorms and that they will need to keep an eye on him when the weather gets bad.

5. She is filled with love for the preacher.

7. He says that there are a lot of thunderstorms in Florida during the summer.

The Big Old Tree (page 36)

1. It is located in the very back of the garden. It has all kinds of bottles (whiskey, wine, beer) hanging from its branches. The bottles clang against each other in the wind.

2. It symbolizes all of the things she has done wrong in her life.

3. She wants Opal to know that she shouldn't judge people by the things they have done in their past. She should look more at the things people are doing now to try to be better.

4. The tree makes her think of her mama. She wonders if her mama thinks about the wrong things she has done and if she ever thinks about her daughter.

The Story of the War (page 39)

1. She is annoyed that Amanda is there. She would rather just share the moment with Miss Franny and Winn-Dixie.

2. the Civil War

3. When she is telling Opal that *Gone with the Wind* is a wonderful book about the Civil War, Opal seems to have never heard of the Civil War.

4. the firing on Fort Sumter

5. Accept appropriate responses, such as "War is hell" and "War should be a cuss word, too."

ANSWER KEY (CONT.)

A Taste of Sorrow (page 41)

Amanda: someone named Carson

Gloria: like people leaving

the Preacher: like melancholy

Otis: like being in jail

Sweetie Pie: like not having a dog

1. *From most sorrowful to least:* her mama left when Opal was small, she had to leave all of her friends in her old town, the Dewberry boys pick on her.

2. She was most surprised by Amanda's reaction. She thought Amanda didn't have anything to be sad about. She learned that Amanda's little brother drowned and died.

Characteristic Reactions (pages 44–45)

The information for the left column of the chart is given below. Accept appropriate responses in the right column of the chart.

Gloria Dump: She seems skeptical at first and asks a few questions, but she agrees to it quickly.

the Preacher: He tells Opal to have fun, but then she informs him that he is coming to the party, too. This gives him pause, as he didn't expect to be invited.

Miss Franny Block: She is immediately excited, and she suggests that Amanda be invited, too.

Amanda Wilkinson: She is nervous and taken aback, but she thanks Opal and accepts the invitation.

Sweetie Pie Thomas: She is very excited, and she immediately tells Opal that the party must have a theme.

Stevie Dewberry: He says no because he doesn't want to go to the witch's house.

Dunlap Dewberry: He smiles and says that he and his brother will come to the party.

Otis: He immediately says he can't go. When Opal tells him he doesn't have to talk to people and he can play his guitar, he changes his mind about going.

Conflicting Feelings (page 46)

1. During the thunderstorm, Winn-Dixie disappears. No one can find him.

Was This Foreshadowed? (page 47)

1. There are many such storms during the summer in Florida.

2. the Preacher

3. Winn-Dixie was running around frantically, terrorized by the thunder and lightning.

5. Gertrude the parrot

Two Timelines (page 51)

Group 1: Opal and her father walk through town looking for Winn-Dixie; Opal worries that he was hit by a car; in her mind, Opal makes a top 10 list of things to remember about Winn-Dixie; the Preacher says they should stop looking, which upsets Opal; Opal yells at her father and accuses him of letting her mama go; Opal's father tells her that he tried to hold onto her mother and he thinks about her every day; Opal's father cries, and Opal comforts him; Opal's father tells her that at least her mama left him one very important thing: her.

Group 2: Gloria convinced the Dewberry boys that she wasn't a witch; the partygoers decided to play music while they waited for Opal and her father to come back; as Otis played music, somebody sneezed from inside the bedroom; they found Winn-Dixie there, hiding under the bed; Winn-Dixie joined the party and fell asleep immediately.

MEETING STANDARDS

The lessons and activities included in *Rigorous Reading: An In-Depth Guide to Because of Winn-Dixie* meet the following Common Core State Standards for grades 3–6. (©Copyright 2010. National Governors Association Center for Best Practices and Council of Chief State School Officers. All rights reserved.)

The code for each standard covered in this resource is listed in the table below and on pages 79–80. The codes are listed in boldface, and the page numbers of the activities that meet that standard are listed in regular type. For more information about the Common Core State Standards and for a full listing of the descriptions associated with each code, go to *http://www.corestandards.org/* or visit *http://www.teachercreated.com/standards/*.

Here is an example of an English Language Arts (ELA) code and how to read it:

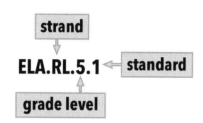

ELA Strands	
L	= Language
W	= Writing
RF	= Reading: Foundational Skills
RL	= Reading: Literature
SL	= Speaking and Listening

✦ ✦

Strand Reading: Literature   **Substrand** Key Ideas and Details

ELA.RL.3.1, ELA.RL.4.1, ELA.RL.6.1: 10–14, 16, 18–19, 22–25, 27–30, 32–36, 38–41, 43–48, 50–51, 58–59, 63, 68–71

ELA.RL.5.1: 14, 16, 19, 22, 25, 27, 29–30, 32, 36, 38–39, 43, 50

ELA.RL.3.2: 11–13, 16–19, 22, 25, 27–28, 30, 32–36, 38–39, 41, 43–46, 48, 50, 59, 68–69

ELA.RL.4.2, ELA.RL.5.2, ELA.RL.6.2: 10–13, 16–19, 22, 25, 27–28, 30, 32–36, 38–41, 43–45, 48, 50–51, 54, 57–59, 68–69

ELA.RL.3.3: 11–13, 16, 18–19, 22–25, 27–30, 32–36, 38–39, 41, 43–48, 50, 58, 60

ELA.RL.4.3: 10–13, 16–20, 22–25, 27–30, 32–36, 38–41, 43–48, 50–51, 58, 60

ELA.RL.5.3: 11–12, 16, 18–20, 22–25, 27–30, 32–36, 38–39, 41, 43–48, 50

ELA.RL.6.3: 10, 12–13, 16–19, 22–25, 27–30, 32–36, 38–39, 41, 43–48, 50–51, 57, 59

Strand Reading: Literature   **Substrand** Craft and Structure

ELA.RL.3.4, ELA.RL.4.4, ELA.RL.5.4, ELA.RL.6.4: 12, 14, 16, 19–20, 22, 24–25, 27–30, 32–36, 38–39, 41, 43–45, 48, 50

ELA.RL.3.5, ELA.RL.5.5, ELA.RL.6.5: 12, 15–17, 22–23, 25, 27–30, 32–36, 38–39, 41, 43–48, 50–51, 53, 57–59

ELA.RL.4.5: 52–53

ELA.RL.3.6: 18, 29, 33, 44–48, 54, 62

ELA.RL.4.6: 62

ELA.RL.5.6: 18, 23, 28, 30, 33–36, 39, 41, 47–48, 62, 68–69

ELA.RL.6.6: 17–20, 23, 28, 30, 33–36, 39, 47–48, 58, 68–69

MEETING STANDARDS (CONT.)

+ +

Strand Reading: Literature   **Substrand** Range of Reading and Level of Text Complexity

ELA.RL.3.10, ELA.RL.4.10, ELA.RL.5.10, ELA.RL.6.10: 10–73

+ +

Strand Reading: Foundational Skills   **Substrand** Phonics and Word Recognition

ELA.RF.3.3, ELA.RF.4.3, ELA.RF.5.3: 8–75

Strand Reading: Foundational Skills   **Substrand** Fluency

ELA.RF.3.4, ELA.RF.4.4, ELA.RF.5.4: 8–75

+ +

Strand Writing   **Substrand** Text Types and Purposes

ELA.W.3.1, ELA.W.4.1, ELA.W.5.1, ELA.W.6.1: 11–19, 21–28, 30–35, 38, 41–43, 46–47, 50, 54–55, 57–59, 60, 62, 68–73

ELA.W.3.2, ELA.W.4.2, ELA.W.5.2, ELA.W.6.2: 8, 10–17, 19–24, 26–47, 49–55, 57–59, 63, 68–72

ELA.W.3.3, ELA.W.4.3, ELA.W.5.3, ELA.W.6.3: 61–63

Strand Writing   **Substrand** Production and Distribution of Writing

ELA.W.3.4, ELA.W.4.4, ELA.W.5.4, ELA.W.6.4: 8, 10–13, 15–16, 20–23, 26–27, 31–38, 40, 42–45, 49–51, 54–55, 57–63, 68–72

ELA.W.3.5, ELA.W.4.5, ELA.W.5.5, ELA.W.6.5: 68–71

Strand Writing   **Substrand** Research to Build and Present Knowledge

ELA.W.3.8, ELA.W.4.8, ELA.W.5.8: 9, 16, 18, 21–22, 26–27, 31–32, 37–38, 42–43, 49–50, 55, 70–71

ELA.W.4.9, ELA.W.5.9, ELA.W.6.9: 10–75

Strand Writing   **Substrand** Range of Writing

ELA.W.3.10, ELA.W.4.10, ELA.W.5.10, ELA.W.6.10: 8–73

+ +

Strand Speaking and Listening   **Substrand** Comprehension and Collaboration

ELA.SL.3.1, ELA.SL.4.1, ELA.SL.5.1, ELA.SL.6.1: 18, 25, 28, 33, 48, 52–53, 64–67

ELA.SL.3.2, ELA.SL.4.2, ELA.SL.5.2, ELA.SL.6.2: 25, 48

ELA.SL.3.3, ELA.SL.4.3, ELA.SL.5.3, ELA.SL.6.3: 25, 48

Strand Speaking and Listening   **Substrand** Presentation of Knowledge and Ideas

ELA.SL.3.4, ELA.SL.4.4, ELA.SL.5.4, ELA.SL.6.4: 64–67

ELA.SL.3.5, ELA.SL.4.5, ELA.SL.5.5, ELA.SL.6.5: 52–53, 66–67

ELA.SL.3.6, ELA.SL.4.6, ELA.SL.5.6, ELA.SL.6.6: 52–53, 64–67

MEETING STANDARDS (CONT.)

+ +

Strand Language   **Substrand** Conventions of Standard English

ELA.L.3.1, ELA.L.4.1, ELA.L.5.1, ELA.L.6.1: 8-73

ELA.L.3.2, ELA.L.4.2, ELA.L.5.2, ELA.L.6.2: 8-73

Strand Language   **Substrand** Knowledge of Language

ELA.L.3.3, ELA.L.4.3, ELA.L.5.3, ELA.L.6.3: 8-75

Strand Language   **Substrand** Vocabulary Acquisition and Use

ELA.L.3.4, ELA.L.4.4, ELA.L.5.4, ELA.L.6.4: 8-75

ELA.L.3.5, ELA.L.4.5, ELA.L.5.5, ELA.L.6.5: 8-75

ELA.L.3.6, ELA.L.4.6, ELA.L.5.6, ELA.L.6.6: 8-75

+ +

NOTES

_____

_____

_____

_____

_____

_____

_____

_____

_____

_____

_____

_____

_____

_____

_____

_____

Made in the USA
Middletown, DE
27 September 2020